TRUCKS

TRAVELING MACHINES

Jason Cooper

Rourke Enterprises, Inc.
Vero Beach, Florida 32964

PHOTO CREDITS

© Lynn M. Stone

LIBRARY OF CONGRESS
Library of Congress Cataloging-in-Publication Data
Cooper, Jason, 1942-
    Trucks / by Jason Cooper.
    p.   cm. — (Traveling machines)
    Includes index.
    Summary: Examines the history, varieties, and special uses
of trucks.
    ISBN 0-86592-491-0
    1. Trucks—Juvenile literature.   [1. Trucks.]   I. Title.
II. Series: Cooper, Jason, 1942-   Traveling machines.
TL230. 15.C66   1991
629.224—dc20   90-26923
                                CIP
                                AC

TABLE OF CONTENTS

TRUCKS

Trucks are motor **vehicles** usually used for transporting freight, or **cargo.** Trucks carry most of the freight in North America. Counted together, trucks carry much more cargo than trains carry.

Trucks are built on a steel frame. The engine and the driver's area, the **cab,** are in the front. The rear of the truck is the cargo area, which is enclosed on some trucks and open on others.

Most trucks are bigger than cars. Trucks are also stronger and more rugged.

Lumber on a flatbed truck

EARLY TRUCKS

The first trucks in North America appeared in the 1890s. They were really cars with a wagon-like area for carrying lightweight loads.

These trucks had steam engines or electric engines, and they had solid rubber tires. Gasoline engines and air-filled tires were introduced in the early 1900s. These improvements allowed trucks to travel faster and farther and carry heavier loads.

During World War I (1914-1918), trucks carried important war supplies.

A 1906 McIntyre "commercial car,"
one of the early trucks

MODERN TRUCKS

Before trucks existed, freight was shipped on land by horse-drawn wagons and trains. By the end of World War I, the United States had 600,000 trucks. During the 1920s, many good highways were built across America. Trucks became important as a way to transport freight.

Today's trucks are powerful and fast. Some have the same comforts as cars. New trucks are bright, colorful, and fairly streamlined.

New trucks aboard an eighteen-wheeler

IN THE SWIM DISCOUNT

SWIMMING POOL SUPPLIES

BATAVIA
406-1707

ELMHURST
832-7946

LIGHT TRUCKS

Modern trucks are often placed in groups based on their loaded weight. Light trucks weigh up to 10,000 pounds. (A heavy automobile weighs about 4,000 pounds.)

Pickups are the best known light trucks. Pickups carry cargo in an open-topped area with steel sides.

Panel trucks are lightweights with enclosed cargo areas. Pleasure vans are panel trucks with windows, carpet, and soft seats.

Some of the smallest trucks weigh less than heavy automobiles.

Panel truck

Heavy duty off-road truck

Fire engine

MEDIUM TRUCKS

Trucks between 10,000 and 20,000 pounds when loaded are medium weight. Most medium-weight trucks are owned by businesses. They haul loads short distances or do special jobs.

Medium-size trucks may carry such things as furniture, glass, chemicals, bottles, packages, and food.

Some of these trucks have **racks** for carrying bottles or glass. Others have open cargo areas called **flatbeds** or box-like cargo areas that may be refrigerated.

Street sweeper

HEAVY TRUCKS

Tankers, cement trucks, dump trucks, and trailer trucks are among the heavyweights of the highways. These trucks with their loads weigh over 20,000 pounds.

Trailer trucks are made up of two units—a tractor, or cab, and a trailer. Some states allow the tractor to pull two trailers at once.

Trailer trucks are also called semitrailers, **semis,** and **eighteen-wheelers.** Trailers usually have eight wheels and tractors have ten.

The largest trucks are too huge to be safe on highways. These are off-road trucks used in **mining.**

Tanker truck

SPECIAL TRUCKS

Some trucks are built for purposes other than hauling. Bucket trucks, for example, lift workers high above the ground. Fire engines are special trucks that carry firefighters, ladders, and hoses. Bookmobiles are libraries on wheels.

Armies have special rugged trucks for carrying soldiers and weapons. Some other special trucks are motor homes, street sweepers, well diggers, and cement mixers.

Cement mixer

TRUCKING

A truck driver who says "I've been everywhere" may be telling the truth. The men and women who drive trucks in North America travel everywhere there are roads. Big trucks haul cargo from one coast to the other.

Trucking is a major industry. About nine million people in the United States work in the trucking industry. Two million of them are truck drivers.

Trucking companies ship almost everything we use, like gasoline, steel, wood, automobiles, food, and other products.

Tractor trailer on an interstate run

THE WONDER OF TRUCKS

The 40 million trucks in North America are among our most useful and important vehicles.

Each day thundering eighteen-wheelers transport thousands of pounds of goods. Smaller trucks perform dozens of other jobs, from rescue and repair to short distance deliveries. Millions of light trucks are family vehicles—part car and part cargo hauler.

The wonder is that for every job, there seems to be a truck built to do it!

Glossary

cab (KAB) — the forward part of a truck that houses the driver and the driver's controls; the forward unit of a trailer truck

cargo (KAR go) — the goods being transported; freight

eighteen-wheeler (AYTEEN WHEE ler) — a trailer truck with eight wheels on the trailer and ten on the tractor (cab) unit

flatbed (FLAT bed) — a flat, platform-like cargo section

mining (MY ning) — the process by which rocks and minerals are taken from the ground

rack (RAK) — a framework to hold certain articles

tanker (TANK er) — a truck on which a tank is mounted to carry liquid, such as oil or milk

vehicle (VEE hih kul) — something which carries or transports

semi (SEH my) — short form of semitrailer; a tractor and trailer rig

INDEX